On the WING

North American Birds 4

Andrea Voon

Richard Han

← 44cm →

Steller's Jay

French: Geai de Steller

Little wings, little wings, flap flap flap…

Voice actors in the forests are on the wing.

Steller's Jays, Steller's Jays, clap clap clap…

Mimic hawks and sounds they hear on the wing.

← 40cm →

← 44cm →

Red-winged Blackbird
French: Carouge à épaulettes

Yellow-headed Blackbird
French: Carouge à tête jaune

Little wings, little wings, flap flap flap…

Border patrols in the marshes are on the wing.

Red-winged Blackbirds, Yellow-headed Blackbirds, clap clap clap…

Defend their territories as they sing.

← 38cm →

Varied Thrush
French: Grive à collier

Little wings, little wings, flap flap flap…

Flute players in the forests are on the wing.

Varied Thrushes, Varied Thrushes, clap clap clap…

Spooky and eerie as they sing.

←33cm→

Say's Phoebe

French: Moucherolle à ventre roux

Little wings, little wings, flap flap flap…

Pest control technicians in the grasslands are on the wing.

Say's Phoebes, Say's Phoebes, clap clap clap…

Snatch insects in midair as they sing.

←32cm→

Barn Swallow

French: Hirondelle rustique

Little wings, little wings, flap flap flap...

Fashion designers in the grasslands are on the wing.

Barn Swallows, Barn Swallows, clap clap clap...

Display their tuxedos as they sing.

Cedar Waxwing
French: Jaseur d'Amérique

←30cm→

Little wings, little wings, flap flap flap…

Masked heroes in the open woodlands are on the wing.

Cedar Waxwings, Cedar Waxwings, clap clap clap

Pick a gift for their lovely wife as they sing.

Purple Finch
French: Roselin pourpré

←26cm→

Little wings, little wings, flap flap flap...

Mounties in the forests are on the wing.

Purple Finches, Purple Finches, clap clap clap...

Crush seeds and extract nuts as they sing.

House Finch

French: Roselin familier

←25cm→

Little wings, little wings, flap flap flap…

Carol singers in the towns are on the wing.

House Finches, House Finches, clap clap clap…

Cheerful and merry as they sing.

<- 23cm ->

Yellow-rumped Warbler
French: Paruline à croupion jaune

Little wings, little wings, flap flap flap…

Belly dancers in the forests are on the wing.

Yellow-rumped Warblers, Yellow-rumped Warblers, clap clap clap…

Dance in the berry bushes as they sing.

American Goldfinch

French: Chardonneret jaune

← 22cm →

Little wings, little wings, flap flap flap…

Potato chip sellers in the open woodlands are on the wing.

American Goldfinches, American Goldfinches, clap clap clap…

Put on their gold suit as they sing.

Black-capped Chickadee

.21cm.

French: Mésange à tête noire

Chestnut-backed Chickadee

.19cm.

French: Mésange à dos marron

Tiny wings, tiny wings, flap flap flap...

Ninjas in the forests are on the wing.

Black-capped Chickadees, Chestnut-backed Chickadees, clap clap clap...

Hide thousands of food items as they sing.

Golden-crowned Kinglet

French: Roitelet à couronne dorée

..18cm.

Ruby-crowned Kinglet

French: Roitelet à couronne rubis

Tiny wings, tiny wings, flap flap flap…

Jewelry appraisers in the forests are on the wing.

Golden-crowned Kinglets, Ruby-crowned Kinglets, clap clap clap…

Conceal their precious crowns as they sing.

Little wings, tiny wings, flap flap flap...

Breeding Papa birds are on the wing.

Little wings, tiny wings, clap clap clap...

Molt into their unique plumages as they sing.

Author

Andrea Voon

Over the past few years, Andrea has learned and grown with her family as a full-time mother in Canada. Back in Malaysia, she was a Chinese immersion elementary school teacher. In 2021, Andrea started her journey as an author. Growing up in a multilingual environment, Andrea loves the beauty of languages on their own. She has the vision to publish picture books to support bilingual families in raising their children in English, Chinese, and Cantonese reading.

Photographer

Richard Han

Richard loves to practice patience through his lenses of the natural world. He enjoys observing the wildlife and photographing the natural lifestyles that animals live. He is excited to present the beautiful photos that he captured in dreamy tones and colors to all the birds lover.

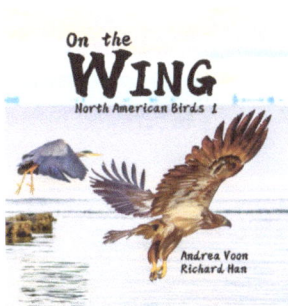

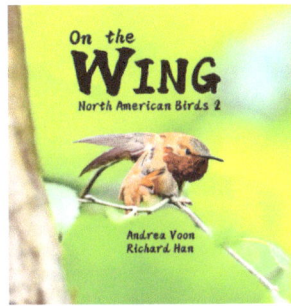

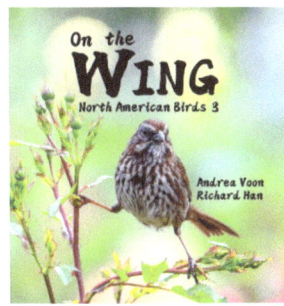

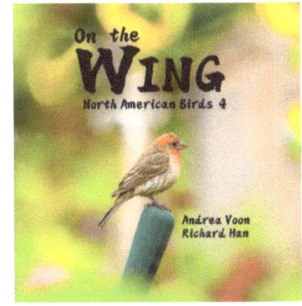

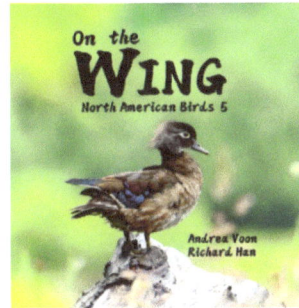

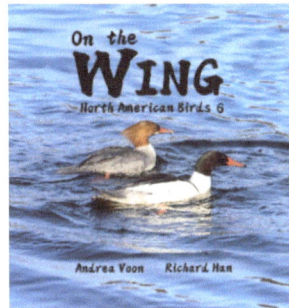

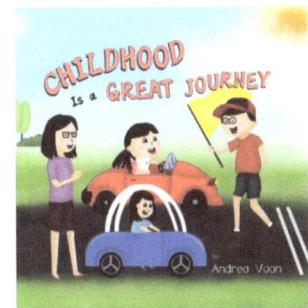

On the **WING**
North American Birds 1
Andrea Voon
Richard Han

On the **WING**
North American Birds 2
Andrea Voon
Richard Han

On the **WING**
North American Birds 3
Andrea Voon
Richard Han

On the **WING**
North American Birds 4
Andrea Voon
Richard Han

EVERY DAY Is a FUN DAY
by Andrea Voon
Illustrated by Yapp Shih Ern

On the **WING**
North American Birds 5
Andrea Voon
Richard Han

On the **WING**
North American Birds 6
Andrea Voon   Richard Han

CHILDHOOD Is a GREAT JOURNEY
by Andrea Voon

To **Shirley Han, Derek, Eliana, Alayna & Magnus Dominus**

with love -- Andrea. V

For **Richard Han**
The patience in natural photography

ISBN 978-1-998856-48-0
Text Copyright © 2024 Andrea Voon
Photo Credit © 2024 Richard Han

Milton Keynes UK
Ingram Content Group UK Ltd.
UKHW051504221024
R3719500002B/R37195PG449816UKX00002B/1